Genre  Historical

MW00475482

**Essential Question**

How do shared experiences help people adapt to change?

# HARD TIMES

by David Murphy
illustrated by Carl Pearce

# CHAPTER 1

# A TOUGH DECISION

"We can't go on like this."

Ruth and Ritchie had just blown out the candle on their birthday cake. It was the twins' twelfth birthday, but it did not feel like a party in the little dining room.

Their father, John Tillerman, spoke from the head of the worn table. The lines on his face had deepened with each letter from the bank. Things were serious.

It was 1933, four years since the Great Depression had begun. Those four years had been desperately hard for the Tillerman family as they battled to scrape a living from their small farm.

"The way I figure it, if we don't do somethin' soon," John continued, "we'll have to pack up and head west, along with a million other poor souls in search of the Promised Land."

Just this morning, the latest in a parade of sorry-looking automobiles had passed by their place with boxes and suitcases roped to their roofs. Ruth had waved, but no one had waved back. They never did.

The stock market crash of October 1929 had spread chaos across America and the rest of the world. All through the Midwest, farmers who could not afford the repayments on their loans were packing up and heading west to California.

"They say there's work at the corn-processing plant," said Martha.

"Can't rely on rumors these days, Ma," John said. "By the time you get to hearin' about it, they coulda filled those jobs many times over. Anyway, it's 30 miles there and back. Gas for the truck would drink every last cent."

Ritchie spoke up. Seeing his father looking so careworn made his stomach ache.

"Mrs. Norris said she'd give Ruth and me 10 cents a week for milking her cows and helping her do other chores after school. I assume that would help," he said.

John looked at the two children and smiled gently. Ruth had straight red hair, freckles, and Martha's blue eyes, while Ritchie's hair was brown and tousled and his eyes a deeper brown. "But it's not just their features that are different," John thought. "Ritchie is the responsible, serious twin, Ruth the impulsive, fiery one."

"Mrs. Norris is bein' real kind," John said finally. "I appreciate the sympathy, but I'd never rest easy if we accepted charity from someone who can't afford it any more than we can."

"I could sell my trumpet," Ritchie offered.

"And I could sell Bridget," Ruth said with a quaver in her voice. Bridget might be slow and a little ornery, but Ruth loved that old mare.

"You'll do no such thing." Martha reached out and took her children's hands. "Things'll get better soon, I guarantee. Playing your music and ridin' Bridget give you kids a lot of pleasure. We all need somethin' to do to take our minds off these hard times."

Martha paused, then added, "I enjoy singing."

She did not mention that she had loved playing the piano too, until they had sold it the year before.

"And your daddy's got his sketching," she continued. "Why, you know he can draw someone's face in the blink of an eye."

"Daddy, I have an idea about how we could make some money," said Ruth.

"Spit it out, then," her father said.

"Why don't you go around to people and offer to draw them? They could pay whatever they could afford."

There was a pause while John gave the idea his usual serious thought. "Clever idea," he said, "and I appreciate your being so supportive, but no one around here has the money to pay for somethin' they don't need."

"I was reading a magazine in the general store. It was all about Chicago," Ritchie broke in excitedly. "It said there were still thousands of rich people there. It said the ladies were dripping with diamonds—dripping! They'd surely want your portraits there, Daddy."

"And what would happen to the farm while I was gone?" said John. "Who'd do all the hard work?"

Ritchie looked glum. He had always done his chores, but without much enthusiasm. He preferred to figure out a new recipe or to play his trumpet. It was Ruth who loved the farm.

Martha had been listening quietly to the discussion.

"The kids' ideas are the best we've had so far, John," she said. "We'd miss you every day, but between the three of us, we could handle the farm work, and it'd just be for a short time."

"But what about somewhere to stay?" John said.

"You could stay at my sister's place. Times are bad for them too, but they won't turn kin away, and you could help out with the rent."

"I don't know, Ma," John said. "Chicago's an awful long way away, and what if somethin' happened?"

"We've got the Norris farm right by, and the kids are gettin' so grown up they'll be a great help. We'll be fine."

"And we'll write to you," Ruth said tearfully. "When you write back, you can tell us all about those fancy rich people and how much they like your pictures."

"Okay," John said, "I'll send money for the bank payments, and I'll write when I can. That's a promise."

# CHAPTER 2

# LIFE WITHOUT DADDY

Four months later, Ruth woke one morning to the sound of crows calling from high in the beech trees. She slid out of bed and dressed quickly. Ritchie was in the kitchen pantry getting flour and eggs to make pancakes.

"Thank goodness he likes to cook!" Ruth thought. She reckoned Ritchie must have been given her share of cooking talent. It seemed that every time she tried to make something, it burned.

Ruth collected the milking pail from outside the back door and headed for the field where Doris, the home cow, was waiting.

"Ma! Breakfast's ready," Ritchie called when Ruth returned.

"Ma's got so thin, and she's looking beat," Ruth thought when her mother came into the dining room. Obviously, Ritchie noticed too, because he piled his mother's plate high with pancakes.

Martha sat at her usual place with Ruth to her left, Ritchie to her right, and the place at the head of the table vacant.

"Another busy day coming up," Martha said. "The nights are gettin' colder, so we need to build up the woodpile. Think you can handle the big saw by yourself, Ruthie? I'd send Ritchie with you, but I need him to help with the roof."

"I'm no weakling, Ma," said Ruth, firing up. "I'm 12 years old."

Martha looked from her son to her daughter. There was Ritchie, neatly assembling his food onto his fork, eating slowly and carefully, and there was Ruth, her plate all a mess, piling food into her mouth as if she hadn't eaten for a month. Ritchie was so calm, and Ruth had a temper that flared at any sign of preference for her twin.

"I'm not assuming that you're weak, Ruthie," Martha said. "I'm very proud of you for pullin' your weight so well. Now, Ritchie, I need you to make some new shingles and then we'll fix up the roof together this afternoon. You think I can nominate you for that job?"

"Reckon so," said Ritchie.

Martha sighed. "And it looks as if the truck might have a gas-line blockage. I'd better fix that first off so I can drive down to the store while you kids get started on your work."

When Ruth went outside after breakfast, she sniffed the air as if it were perfume. She loved the outdoors and life on the farm. She knew the names of all the flowers in the woods around their place and was learning the names of different birds.

Ruth took an apple over to Bridget, collected the saw from the barn, and set out for the back field.

John had felled some beech trees before he left and had hauled one log onto the sawbuck in a clearing at the edge of the woods. Ruth looked at the big log resting in the notch on the sawbuck. Then she gripped the big saw with both hands.

An hour later, there was a pile of logs at Ruth's feet that were the right size for the stove. The September sun was blazing down, and Ruth was hot and her hands felt raw. There was a stream nearby in the woods where she could wash her face, have a drink, and take a rest.

When she reached the stream, Ruth hitched up her dress, crouched down, and cupped her hands to scoop up the ice-cold water. Then she heard a strange noise and thought, "It sounds like a baby playing with … a rattle!" She looked up. There on the other side of the stream, its long body coiled, its tongue flicking, its eyes fixed on her, was a rattlesnake.

Back at the house, Ritchie heard the scream. He dropped his ax and dashed toward the sound. "Ruthie! Ruthie!"

When he found her, she was kneeling, her body rigid but shaking with fright. The rattlesnake was no more than five or six feet away. Every few seconds, its tail made a deathly sound.

"Stay very calm," Ritchie whispered, placing his hands on Ruth's shoulders. "Stand up and step back slow as you can. Rattlers don't attack unless they feel threatened. She's probably protecting some eggs. Just lean back against me. It's gonna be fine."

Ruth and Ritchie backed away until they reached a bend in the trail, and then they turned and ran back to the house.

"Gosh, Ritchie, how'd you know what to do?" asked Ruth when they had reached the kitchen and she had gathered her breath.

"I read about rattlesnakes in Daddy's almanac," said Ritchie. "When they're going to strike, they open their jaws and form their bodies into curves. That one was coiled up with its head on its body. The rattle was just telling you to stay away."

"You saved my skin," said Ruth.

"Nah, it was nothin'."

At supper that evening, Martha frowned when she heard the story. "Well," she said after a few seconds' thought, "I guess it all worked out. We won't tell your daddy, though."

# CHAPTER 3

# TOGETHER AGAIN

Finally, the day they had been looking forward to for weeks had arrived. It was Thanksgiving, and for the first time since he had left for Chicago, John Tillerman was coming home.

Ritchie and Martha had gone all out to create a feast. They couldn't manage a turkey, but there was roast chicken, and Ritchie had dreamed up something he called "Variations on a Potato Theme by Richard Tillerman." Martha's famous apple pie sat under a cloth, ready to go into the oven when the chicken came out.

It was late morning when the Chicago bus pulled over on the main highway and came to a stop with a hiss of brakes.

When John stepped down with his small suitcase and a big canvas bag, he was engulfed. Martha, Ruth, and Ritchie threw their arms around him, and they all held on tightly. The Tillermans were together again at last! After a long moment, they piled into the truck and headed up the road to the farm.

After lunch, they opened the presents John had brought. There was a battered mute for Ritchie's trumpet, a book for Ruth, and material for Martha to make a new dress.

"A trumpet player named Louis Armstrong gave me the mute," said John. "He was playing at one of the clubs on the South Side. I drew his portrait, and he said to me, 'Hey, fella, that's some mighty fine skill you got there.' I told him about you, Ritchie, and he gave me his mute plus five aces."

"What're five aces?" asked Ruth.

"An ace is a dollar bill. I picked up all kinds of slang on Chicago's South Side. *Baloney* means nonsense, and when somethin's real fine, it's *snazzy* or the *cat's meow.*"

"Do you make much money?" asked Ritchie.

"Not much," John said. "Sometimes I jus' get nickels and dimes, sometimes a dollar or two."

"Enough to come back home?" asked Ruth.

"I've been thinking on that, Ruthie," said John. "Being apart has been hard for all of us, and the Depression is showing no sign of coming to an end. I reckon we should all move to Chicago. Your aunt's happy for us to share with her until we get settled."

Martha nodded and said, "Your daddy and I have been writin' about it. When things get better, there's a chance the farm will still be waiting for us, but what matters most right now is that we're all together."

"I don't want to move," Ruth said. "I love it here—I love the fields and the birds and the woods. I love Doris and Bridget—I even love the rattlesnakes."

John frowned. "What rattlesnakes?"

"Oh, Ruthie had a little encounter," Martha said quietly. "It's nothin'."

"Tell me about it," John insisted.

After he heard Ruth's story, he said, "You kids did really well, but that fixes it. The farm needs all of us to run it, but I need to be in Chicago now. We'll all move, and then we'll all come back."

"Ritchie had another idea about earning some money," Ruth said.

"A cookbook for the hard times," said Ritchie.

"Sounds promisin'," said John. "What do you reckon it'd sell for?"

Ritchie thought for a moment. "At least an ace."

"Oh dear," said Martha. "I can see Chicago's going to be a whole new ball game."

## Summarize

Use the most important details from *Hard Times* to summarize the story. Your graphic organizer may help you.

## Text Evidence

1. What features of the text help you identify this story as historical fiction? **GENRE**

2. Compare and contrast Ritchie and Ruth, who are twins but who are very different. **COMPARE AND CONTRAST**

3. On page 15, Martha says moving will be "a whole new ball game." What does this expression mean? Use context clues to figure out the meaning. **IDIOMS**

4. Write to compare and contrast Ruth and Ritchie's reactions to the rattlesnake. How do their reactions reflect their personalities? **WRITE ABOUT READING**

**Compare Texts**
Read about the music scene in Chicago during the 1930s.

# CHICAGO: JAZZ CENTRAL

In the story *Hard Times*, John Tillerman meets Louis Armstrong, one of the greatest jazz trumpet players of all time. Armstrong moved from New Orleans to Chicago in 1922 as part of what is known as the Great Migration.

Between 1910 and 1930, the African American population in the northern states grew by about 40 percent. In the north, there was less discrimination, people could find better schools for their children, and growing industries meant there were more job opportunities.

The prospect of work drew many talented musicians to Chicago. They brought with them a style of music called jazz that had developed in New Orleans. It was a mix of blues, ragtime, and church music.

Louis Armstrong recorded hit after hit for five decades.

17

The popularity of jazz grew quickly. Between 1915 and 1929, there were more than 40 jazz clubs on Chicago's South Side.

Then the Great Depression struck. With fewer people going out to clubs, musicians lost their jobs. Louis Armstrong was one of many who left for New York City, although he still played in cities across the United States, including Chicago. People burned old records to keep warm, and musicians struggled for survival along with everyone else.

Things took a slight turn for the better in the mid-1930s. The Depression still gripped America and people had little money for clubs, but radio brought music to them. No one was more popular with listeners than Benny Goodman and his big band, which played a variation on jazz, called swing.

## JAZZ AND HIP-HOP

People have called jazz "the hip-hop of its day." Both musical styles came out of poor African American urban communities. Jazz was fast, wild, and so different from previous music that it unsettled people. Hip-hop, with its loud bass and angry lyrics, also made some people nervous.

At first, each form of music was only played within those African American urban communities, but later on, other people came to appreciate the music. Now people all over the world listen to jazz and hip-hop.

Swing was fast and lively and fun to dance to—just the sort of music to raise people's spirits in hard times. Millions of people who had never listened to jazz before began filling ballrooms again to dance the Susy Q, the Big Apple, and the Lindy Hop.

Over time, other music styles also emerged from jazz, including rock and roll, rhythm and blues, and pop. Jazz is still very popular today, and Chicago remains a thriving music center.

Swing music was especially popular with teenagers.

## Make Connections

How did people in Chicago adapt to the changes in the economy in the 1930s? ESSENTIAL QUESTION

Compare the role of art for John in *Hard Times* with the role of music for players such as Louis Armstrong in *Chicago: Jazz Central*. How did their skills help them when times were hard? TEXT TO TEXT

## Genre

**Historical Fiction** Historical fiction tells stories about people or events from the past. Historical fiction might include real or made-up characters and events. The details, including dialogue, are usually invented. Like other forms of fiction, historical fiction has a setting, characters, and a plot.

**Read and Find** On page 2 of *Hard Times*, the author tells us when the story is set. On page 14, John uses idiomatic phrases common at that time. The illustrations show us the setting, the way people dressed, and some of the items they used every day. The plot involves John Tillerman's going to Chicago to find work, a common event in the 1930s.

### Your Turn

Working with a partner, compare features of daily life in the 1930s that you have read about in *Hard Times* with your life now. List features that are the same and features that are different. Now imagine that your family has traveled back in time and has to adapt to living in the 1930s. Using your list, draw three cartoons that show your modern family living in the 1930s. For example, you might draw your family looking under the furniture and in closets for a TV, which was not available in the United States in the 1930s. Write a caption for each cartoon to explain what the cartoon shows.